KILL, CRY, OR DIE

A collection of Poems,
Epigrams, Aphorisms, Philosophy,
Thoughts and Humor

PETER A MULLER

Kill, Cry, or Die
Copyright © 2021 by Peter A Muller

All rights reserved. No part of this publication may be reproduced, distributed, or transmitted in any form or by any means, including photocopying, recording, or other electronic or mechanical methods, without the prior written permission of the author, except in the case of brief quotations embodied in critical reviews and certain other non-commercial uses permitted by copyright law.

ISBN
978-1-956161-55-7 (Hardcover)
978-1-956161-54-0 (Paperback)
978-1-956161-53-3 (eBook)

Table of Contents

Chapter 1	Poems	1
Chapter 2	Epigrams, Aphorisms, Thoughts, and Humor	33
Chapter 3	Philosophy and Related Matters	49
Chapter 4	Psychological	57
Chapter 5	God and Religion	63
Chapter 6	Short Stories	67

CHAPTER 1
POEMS

NIGHT ON THE RIVER

Cold night on the Klamath River, editing and writing, what I plan to deliver.
For a year, I did not stir nor quiver. Not a word wrote, not a feeling felt.
It was the death card, I thought, I had been dealt.
In a cocoon, I guess is how I feel, but as I type I think this could be real.
Oh, what a deal. If I can seal my name in the books next to the likes of Voltar.1
Will I go so far as that I can touch a star?
When all I want is a new car, not to go very far.
Then will there be a scar?
From lack of recognition it can't be worse than my condition.
So with my poems I'll be fish'n for people to listen.

---

1 Voltaire

KILL, CRY, OR DIE

It burns inside
And there's never one you can tell
That a jaded heart and weak stomach never shared
This body well.
So when asking yourself to kill, cry, or die,
I roll my eye and sigh,
Because I do all three so very well.

RIDDLE

A riddle for a tune to play on a fiddle;
Oh, how it breaks, when it's oh so brittle.
This trial is a farce. I'm up for acquittal.
You tittle and tattle about all my steps of prattle.
Thrown into battle, rode under saddle.
I'm older than leather for your pleasures of pleather.
From where do you start? From where do you measure?
Heather for heights; feather for flights.
White for rice, green for good, for smoke it you should.
The botanical is a mechanical way
to sense a path astray.
Think about where to jump. Think about where to stay.
Think, don't pray, or you will itch like hay.
To ask for help, to admit to dismay,
to receive something good,
solid like wood.
Knock twice for luck
for every missed duck
that lead to "Oh, fuck!"

TOY AND PLAY

Toy and play and be left that way,
Never forgetting the day,
That glance, had sent the mind into sway
Before, things got kept by dismay.
A few hearts, caught in the system,
Somebody's got to pay.
For that is the way, at least for the day.
Dreams are of the change for which we all pray.
"Can I have it my way?"
But good friends:
"I must say these great travels, travel but one way."
How long does a passenger sit before sent into fray?
Better be rewarded for all the frustrations afforded
Or the feelings of heart jade when deported.
To that old lonely place where one sits to face the
Thoughts that were recorded, Organized, traced and
Sorted.
So, when next faced, we'll thwart it.

WIND

As the winds blow,
Poems rest, riding the flow,
Laughing and crying while always on the go.
Lost and found from mouth to ear.
Waiting to reappear
And arise to your hear.
When out on life's lonely peer,
Its spell offers solace from fear.
Always a delight to have one near.
When you need high noon at night, write it bright
Or put out the light with a spit and fight.
Exercise on things of fright:
Crumble the mighty it just might,
Weigh heavy on the soul
Who paid its toll.
To pass as words blow
Through the charge of the wind.

DESIRE

This world's not mine.
But my desires are my own,
The fire that heats my heart's home.
Not a fret or regret for a misplaced bet,
It's the undone that haunts and taunts,
It's the kiss never felt.
The way lonely eyes melt.
That when felt and had
Gives moments not sad
And see that it's not so bad.

SEBASTIAN

My cat is always on his back,
Which prompts me to attack his belly.
While it shakes like jelly,
While he weighs like a sack of potatoes,
He don't eat no tomatoes.
Always in the same pose
Until you turn on the vacuum hose.
Then rose to flee.
So often, find him up a tree,
So high that you cannot see.
So, I sport a frown till he comes down
With a thud he will land. Not accepting my hand.
But he likes to demand that I open the door;
Then he's out to explore the terrain.
And that's where he'll remain
Until it starts to rain
And he can no longer stay out.
So, he's got to come in
And make me grin.
When I see him all wet,
He's such a sweet pet.

SATIRE

Satirical for sure:
Surreal for certain. It lurks behind every curtain.
Who do you think it's hurtin'?
Day to day, through every door,
A teardrop in the rain becomes one more.
To make a hit it takes something other than spit
Puddled up by those that quit.

RAINBOW

I followed a rainbow and found a pot of shit
And called it gold but gold got old and refuses to fold.
And I'm not nearly old and sick of being told to go for the gold.
If someone listened, then it was me you told.

AMOUS

Two sides to a coin but that's a nickel and this is a dime
Don't be a cop if ya don't want to commit a crime.
Now that I'm clean nature thinks I'm covered in grime.
And when I sit, I can't stand the time,
But time don't stand.
So, wake me up when this train hits land.
As the fish jumped for his first breath, he proclaims:
"My name is Amous. When I hit land,
Some son of a bitch is going to make me famous."
And the lion, he just barks at the sea.

GLORY

When the empty inside is the face
You wear outside, there is nothing you can consume.
To make sense of resume with no use for a broom
Already, swept aside by life's boom,
I wonder if I should accept doom. I can't help but exit the room.
These boxes don't match my round face.
Never failing to be out of place,
Where are you going? Can I run at your pace?
Our thoughts are the only things that belong in space;
But what the hell, it's the thrill of the chase
That keeps us running in this race.
So, have a seat while I tell you a story,
Of how the emptiness came after the glory.

RELATIONS

It's not torture; its training.
Or did you call life's vaccination the game
Begging for the ball and chain to remain?
After all, how can one not know when it's all the same.
Wise to what will remain, pick and choose the
poison, the pain,
And always be quick to avoid the frame.
After all, what was the choice? What is the blame?
Stories have been planted about my name.
Erase this mark from my face
Or it will be your greatest disgrace.
I'm up for a jog, will it be a race?
Run and jump when things go thump;
Scream and roar when you want more.
Priceless, the heart, not poor.
An endless place to explore as one hand holds the door.
When things get sore,
There are just some things not taken no more.
Manners is core.
Tasteless for the tasteful
Oh, once again, disgrace can infect the place.
It all leaves its trace;

Call the inspector for we've got a case
Of spit for mace, malice at dawn,
When the bomb spun its song.
If you're brave, come along.
To the march of meet when trampled by feet.
Bought and sold by deceit
Never knowing what is defeat.
Look, there's a hole; we have sprung a leak.
This time we've got what we seek;
Why, oh, why must one always speak?
That's about it, a peak.
A high vision to see or a place where it's had
Does not want to be.
Sometimes, I forget, what's my decree?
I'm who I'll be.
Step outside if you have got to piss for not even its smell
Will be missed when the infinite offers such bliss.
The magic show, one never to miss.
By god, what's in that kiss that lights the carnival?
Oh, how the dance of the stone statues did fall.
The fire that took what the ice did keep,
The power of weep.
When absence can cause the creeps
What method of time is played by the meeks?
The tick and the tock of the wanted rock,
Hit like a sock to the jaw.

A symphony did fall into play,
And all said: "Yay, for today and tomorrow be as it may."
If I have something to say,
I got this crazy little way,
To move and fall into the groove.
Just a fun thing, not a thing to prove.
Who knows with improve?
It's something of sooth
When things go smooth.
Facts were the racks of the hangman,
Who saw the slip in the plan.
This world is crazy. If you're not, it would faze me,
Amaze me, amuse and want to bruise;
Put on the sunglasses.
We're going for a cruise to listen for the news,
With many tools to use. I'll leave the fuse.
For never go first, a burst for the worst,
The never forgotten curse.
Sick for a nurse, an exorcism for things to disperse.
Oh, how some things cost deep in the purse.
Who's who? Who's worse?
Who's best? The one not like the rest;
The lord does jest; don't hold it to your chest
For sometimes there's rest.

DARK

Darkness may carry light within its spaces, but light
Does not carry darkness within it.
Light always travels in its true shape and form while
Darkness needs light in order to have form.
Darkness is omnipresent nothing with virtually no
Traceable source.
Light can just about always be traced to a place of
emission.
Darkness travels faster than light for it is already
there.

STRIDE

I take it all in stride and not flex out of pride,
But with a pen and paper I glide.
As the images start to blur, sometimes you might
Say: "He is a her"
But that's only something of slur.
Of the speech 'cus I got something to tear into that peach and when I preach,
It should be something of teach.

GRAY SHADOW

A shade of gray, a shadow of silk as white as milk,
To the left and in hilt until the situation starts to tilt.
But from the right hand, I was built to be stout, not stilt
And with words, one can get kilt and have to shift
through the silt.
To uncover a shiny thing to discover, with only
Ashes to uncover,
Dusted off to something I'll lover,
But me she must smother and I'll be a smoothie.
That's more than a movie.
Hey, get me high and I get groovy.
So who'll be next to be my soup?
Seesaw but I still ain't seen it all
But a good grip to catch on to a fall.
Into the mist and in the end never pissed
But not all things missed for one that wants to aim
for bliss.
After being blighted, it's alrighted 'cus ya learned
how to fight it.

FARMS

Yikes! I put my love to sleep and now alone I must weep.
If only, one more time, her legs I could sweep into
my arms with no alarms,
With the cat safe from harms.
Purring in the corner and into our life, casting charms.
If you want a lot of animals, you got to live near farms
With barns for brisk nights for hoofed feet
That beat the path of the trail to a lake,
Where we end all our tales.
To start anew when the next ones threw;
But who knew you would know of a good place
to go,
Where a stone one need not throw

MANIC

I've thrown my best poem to the fire.
For under a spell, that would, surely expire.
Something lovely took its course to the flames,
And regret is what remains.
For I held only one copy.
When I try to recall, it only sounds sloppy,
For after the first line, it turns to jalopy.
If only, I had not mis-stashed its only known copy.
Among the coloring books of a mental ward,
Of which to return I could not afford.
But still without it I will seek this award
For I've got many a sword.
With swipes of the pen, I will amend as I pretend;
It's just a drop in the bucket
Like stories from Nantucket.

SOLDIERS OF WAR

The soldiers of war; we love to adore.
Some flex with pride, while others want to hide;
For the ride was no glide and bumpier than a slide.
Some sneer, when inquisitors come near.
For they have felt true fear,
Closer than needing to hear that they did a good job
And that they are no slob
Through the shrapnel, they did weave and bob.
Crawl so nice through fields of rice,
A few of them even had to eat mice.
To make it, they did not fake it,
And now that they are back, some can't take it.
Some got a rake and a kid and a backyard for a bid
As, they tell a story of nightmares of glory,
But, really, it was just gory.
It has lost its alluring features that fill my brain with
Creatures that are scary;
In my dreams things get hairy.
Sometimes we fail and bite the nail;
Rise from sleep, with memories to keep,
And for the dead we weep.
Because in time we've made a leap
To the present, where to be alive is a present.
Though some live like a peasant, others are pleasant
But they all carry the scar of being in a land so far.

SABRINA

My cat is always on the roof,
Getting into acts uncouth;
Why just the other day she bit me with her tooth.
All she knows is violence as she comes creeping
Through the silence.
Then with a pang, you will feel her fang.
In pain I sang out into a shout, that she better get out of my way
As I reach for the spray to keep her at bay.
During the day, she is off to catch prey,
But through it all I must say she is still a ray
Of sunshine
And I'm glad to call her mine.

AGING

In intellect there is insanity.
As I get older, I spare my profanities.
I've learned to keep my thoughts at ease.
Rather stay silent then speak to please.
I can make a good living with a moderate amount of cheese.
I don't spend to pretend that life's woes it will amend.
Every so often, I will speak to an old friend and dust off a memory.
And say: "Hey, remember when we used to explore this earth with curiosity since birth?" Now I'm just paying the rent and no longer get bent but I burn and that makes my lungs a chief concern, for there is nothing better than a good meal and a quick death.

FISH

Like the parts of a fish in oil, this earth is rich.
And because of it you can always get a job digging
a ditch for a dyke,
For we like to take a hike.
And catch a pike, so many fish, and they don't look
alike
but sorta the same like me and my friend Mike.

IMPLY

Sometimes you have to leave it to implication
For the explanation to be in the form of simplification
But when misunderstood, leads to a deviation of attention
Towards what you want to mention.
When left in suspension, you can feel apprehension
For the details when the implied fails
But without it we would have long, drawn out tales.

SHARED LIES

Our truths were based in a foundation of lies.
So that's why I don't trust those guys,
Who work for profit and tell you to listen to the prophet.
He is not relevant and his sermon is not benevolent.
I'd rather study on the intelligence of an elephant
Then pitch a tent and call it holy and preach about guacamole.
To believers that say we've got nothing in common with beavers.
This all just serves as our social structure deceivers.

SEEKER

I was a seeker that sought
Till I fought with the edge
And found that it curved into a wheel.
Try to steal what comes around you, and the big things are sure to confound you.
Can't get away for it surrounds you.
You carry it within;
You just can't throw it in a bin.
So you argue about the sin you never had
And how to get glad,
When more times than not you often feel sad.
Or get mad when you try to grab a hold
And only put your arms into fold.
It did not even help when you were bold because you were only confident in what you were told and sold.
For the price of your ear, they will tell you all of what you want to hear,
But now I'm near from not looking took it away when my brain got to cooking.
Burnt up I live in fertile ash, hardly act rash, other than eating unhealthy stuff like corn beef hash.

LAMB'S BREAD

I smoke lamb's bread to get a good head.
Even though the hairs are not red, it's still good smoke from the Rasta dread.
It's a sativa keeps me up and not puts me in bed.
Smoke it yourself till then, nuff said.

MEMORY

Memory leads to misery.
When pondering one often wants for some sort of wizardry,
To change and rearrange as they ponder their past.
They feel they will be free at last
But only to cast
The shadow so heavy
That it never gets off the ground
For it cannot exist in the air of possibility.
My lack of constant memory is my source of tranquility.

CONTRADICTION

I write the new cliches of contradiction
I learn the truth by reading lots of fiction
To study the past is to make to make a prediction
when it comes to man you can expect lots of friction
from fracking the earth
with no chance given at birth
homogenized cream can't rise to the top
do what you want until comes the cop
than your lucky if all you have to do is stop
but can't chase the people that poison the crop.

LOBOTOMY

I like to write of dichotomy
but must be careful of a reemergence of the lobotomy
they want to find the speck in my brain that won't
let me stand in line
with everyone that is keeping good time
with no use of the talent of rhyme
all there new music has become such a crime
they try to breed us with the brain of a barnacle
to stay stuck to there hull of lies
they are inbred
and want you dead
if you can't dig or dance
that will be your only chance.

CHAPTER 2

EPIGRAMS, APHORISMS, THOUGHTS, AND HUMOR

- The longer recorded history goes on the harder it becomes to have an original thing to say.
- It is easy to see that even a blind man gets upset when you poke him in the eye.
- It's best to be lucky but best not count on luck.
- The richest people usually have family or no one for partners. Partnership between friends never seems to last.
- An explanation does not always equal excusable.
- Most sleepless nights rest in the cradle of desire.
- Bullshit sellers are publicly obligated to buy it.
- Would you rather share laughter or tears?
- Think about how many times you have fallen and then think about how many times you were picked back up. Was it every time?
- Does anyone think the sun is lazy? If so, do they consider water to be lazy? I mean the two that do all for us just sit around.
- The passion to stay alive needs no fuel from emotion.
- Sharing is caring, and when you share, you show that you care not to be alone.
- Saying one wrong thing sets you back ten right things said.
- The problem with counterculture is that it's a culture of its own.
- Epigrams are brilliance born of a poet's laziness.

- I don't know why they bother shooting the people that speak out. It's not like anyone is listening more than half the time.

- What keeps me lost is the thought that everyone else is found.

- Even after you run out of things for others to teach you, there is still a lot left to learn.

- Narrow is the path but broad is the journey.

- Trees are a life of listening.

- There is a thin line between smart and crazy because they are both one out of 100.

- Nothing is quite as noxious as someone whose only goal of every conversation is to say that you are wrong and try to change your mind when they never had a well formed point of view to begin with.

- You may have proved to be different then a monkey but the monkey also proved to make for more charming company.

- A whole lot of darkness can give one an appreciation for the little bit of light a flame casts.

- Love is the feeling of oneness realized through another.

- A person should stay up long enough to see the stars before lying down to sleep.

- Life is a hard lesson to learn and you're paying for the class.

- Choose not to hide behind blind eyes that can see.

- Restless in wait at the invisible gate. Tempting eyes look upon a fate wanted Felt for the ice to melt in the seat that's been dealt.

- Sometimes acting senseless seems so sensible.

- If you need a fire, what good is a log without the kindle to start it?

- Writing is the hardest work you can do to avoid doing hard work.

- Being able to pee standing up comes at the price of missing the bowl from time to time.

- If you beat yourself up over life, you're just going to get twice the beatings life offers.

- A master of mystery does not master all his mystery, for he needs them to walk the road of destiny, one foot in front of the other.

- Our thoughts are not private, but we have been blessed into being able to think as if they are.

- An imagination is a basic issue item given to all. It is just the choice of using it or not.

- Paperwork is the foundation of reality and it is a written memory of words gone past.

- It does not do oneself any good to have their imaginations overwhelmed by another, and that is why there can be too much TV and movies.

- A person with poor imagination imagines the realistically tangible, but there is something to be said about the genius of practicality.

- Even a good past is not a good place to dwell, but it is well for a story to tell.

- Winning is half the battle, and how you play is the other half.

- If you asked a man that was a millionaire what he wanted to be and he told you he wanted to be a millionaire, what would you have to say about that?

- Wits are not common sense but feelings are something we sense and all have in common.

- When throwing stones best to aim for a lake not a mirror.

- At what point do you know you have been someplace long enough to decorate?

- Independent contractors want to be paid better than employees but treated like customers.

- Abandon all hope for a better yesterday.

- I write stuff down, so that anytime I think I got it all figured out, I can read about the last time I had a clue and discover that I really don't know what I am talking about, and the others around me know even less.

- There is plenty of time to put a puzzle together while in a mental ward. I'd hate to do one now and wear the task out and have nothing to pass the time with once inside.

- Some people hold on to their words simply to lure you into wanting to hear them.

- All good lies have their roots firmly planted in truth but beware the bitter aftertaste of false fruit.

- Beware of those who speak for the dead.

- When you use the word *love* like it is going out of style, it loses its fashion.

- When you fall off your high horse, you make a great platform for somebody else to climb up on theirs.

- It is staggering all the things we learn, my only saving grace is my ability to forget it.

- Some people only know how to listen with their mouth.

- Dumb people are interesting in that they will believe anything yet you can't tell 'em nothing.

- Still looking for someone to blame, a typical story that's more of the same, a soul prepared to be maimed.

- Get between a dog and a meal then tell me how friendship did feel.

- The value of being cynical is buying into it when you need to.

- Part of being humble is admiring all the work that goes into an evil plan.

- Does the one eyed man cry twice as much or half as much?

- Are you just killing time or is time killing you?

- Honor yourself only when acting humble and then there is no need.

- The cold leaves no one completely unemployed for everyone is given the task of warming up.

- The best litigators can win both sides of the case.

- Light lives, while darkness just is.

- We are all unwilling participants with free will inside this crazy universe.

- "I will see when I can see," said the blind man, "but for now a cool breeze and warm fire will do."

- No one ever says "Reap what you sow" when the outcome is positive.

- It's easier to walk on water once it is frozen.

- Advice only becomes advice once it is passed on.

- It's easier to forgive a misdeed then to forgive someone for having a misdemeanor character.

- The best way to receive forgiveness is to not make a habit of unforgivable acts.

- If to plunge into darkness is foolish then none be more fool than light.

- Someone that has been hit by a rock does not need faith to know that it's going to hurt if it happens again.

- If love is all good, then can it be good to love something bad?

- When you are honest about your feelings then you always have the right things to say about them.

- A writer that keeps half his pages blank gives you half of everything and half of nothing, for there is power in the potential of an unwritten page.

- For every fad, there is a crowd waiting to adopt it.

- The unseen part of every picture is the person who took it.

- I once set my hand on fire for a dollar and after the experience, I can say that it was a rough way to make a living.

- The vast majority of water is too deep for you to stand in.

- Only visit a cannibal's house after they are doing the dishes for the night.
- Just because it comes in a bowl does not mean you have to eat it with a spoon.
- It takes discipline to keep your house clean when you are surely expecting no company.
- What's the speed of infinity? For it must take forever to get there.
- It does not take a bold man to make a bold statement.
- Before forever ends tell me where it begins.
- Just because you fail to expose a lie does not make the lie true.
- After you fall off mount ego, you land on humble hill.
- Even weeds can grow flowers.
- Wisdom is often painfully learned but when spoken means no harm.
- Even a bugler has died in combat.
- Go far in life but hopefully not too far in the wrong direction.
- Love and hate share qualities with obsession.
- The wise are known to have lived foolish, while the foolish have been known to ignore the wise.
- Your shadow records virtually all your movements but none of the efforts.
- No past meal fills you up when you are hungry now, and learned knowledge is only as good as your memory.

- Some writing is like a friendly loan in that they contain no interest.

- A good cup of tea can make anyone feel like a sage.

- The stars touch with one another's light.

- Most people turn a blind eye toward themselves.

- Hippies are the dirtiest people that still have high regard toward their fashion.

- I enjoy sanity. Unfortunately, it is not one of my stronger suits.

- Ideas are seemingly infinite while good ones are finite.

- I want to remember when life was in the moment and dreams were a promise with little need for hope.

- I feel genius is mostly based on observations and how well they can be translated.

- If you add an odd number to itself, you get an even number. If you add an even number to itself, you get an even number. Odds and evens are never really even, even though the math adds up.

- After they are done whipping you they put the whip in your hand.

- Walking through life is like walking through grass at night. You only avoid stepping in shit by the grace of God.

- A blanket in the sand is how the roads were paved.

- Things are never going your way if a woman punches you in the arm when only the face will do.

- Nothing can be as insulting as the truth.

- Never ask for a pat on the back. Forced praise is praise you don't want.

- All avid book readers dream of being writers.

- When you do not desire something, it is the effect of having what other people think they are going to get out of something.

- Our thoughts are the influence of everything but ourselves. For we hardly control our own thoughts; they just occur.

- The premise of a lot of conversations is "Hey, I was talking to myself and thought you might want to listen in."

- New homeowners are easy to shop for they need everything.

- I talk to myself because I bother to listen more than most people would.

- Just as people have talents, they have stupidity as well. Few to none are good at everything.

- If I ever get famous, I will at least be quotable; for when evaluating history, a summary will do.

- If you can't know it all, then you're a shy step away from knowing nothing and either way, you still must live.

- I don't have a high opinion of myself, but I do know I have a low opinion of others.

- You can take care of all your problems of internal origin but external problems will still find you.

- When you don't have anything new to say, you can say the same old thing to different people.

- Everyone has crazy thoughts. What makes a person crazy is believing them, and the degree of delusion is just a question of imagination and creativity.

- Pain is the only serious problem in the world. Just about all others can be sorted out in your head.

- Although, larger men take up less space than women.

- Most good times are not worth the effort.

- Upholding a principle usually means denying a natural instinct.

- The world is a shared illusion with physical density.

- I have been publicly reserving my opinion until it is for sale.

- The grim reaper may not be God but he can get you a little closer.

- You don't have to like something to be able to do it but you must like it to do it well.

- You break your own heart with expectations outside yourself.

- Since we are all spirits, any form of enlightenment can be spiritual enlightenment. Those who strive for it are like hamsters running a wheel. They get great exercise but don't really get any further than any other hamster in the cage. Take time to let the mind wander and wind up in the strangest of places.

- We are all one in that we come from the same source. Much like the individual hairs that come from the head to form a ponytail.

- A shadow is a form of darkness that would not exist without light.

- We are all outlines in the canvas of the universe and are all related for we are drawn on the same thing.

- We are ourselves when in seclusion for when in seclusion, there is nothing to bear influence on you and no one for you to impress your thoughts upon, so they are in a natural state. Good writing can come from this state of seclusion.

- How many nothings can you count?

- Lay your thoughts to rest on paper and then be able to forget and be free of them, for their retention has been already been handled.

- When there is a disagreement, there is potential for someone to be learning something.

- Loyalty is often bound to disappointment.

- People tend to talk more about their memories then their tomorrows.

- Unarmed people don't get shot nearly as much as an armed person does.

- If most people are their true selves when drunk, than most people are truly obnoxious.

- The cradle of civilization is still in its infancy when it comes to acting civilized.

- No one respects your hunger as much as fast prey.

- Many a talented men had to spend time arguing a myth then spend the extra time on breaking new ground.

- The moment someone has to beg, there soon will be a moment when they curse you. If not overtly then surely secretly. You resent anyone you had to beg from.

- We are mainly just separated by two things. One is the propensity of our thoughts and then the bodies we inhabit.
- By the time you have seen it all, you will have forgotten more than half of it.
- Our foundation of truth is based on a history of lies.
- A principle is only fair when the withholder suffers on account of it.
- To carry another person's opinion is a burden.
- When you change your opinion on a matter, it is usually for the better, for it comes with more understanding.
- Most people like to entertain themselves by annoying others. So, this makes most people, inherently annoying.
- The truth should sound familiar for we are likely to have heard and denied it at some point.
- Trust is a gamble. Place it in no one and bet on yourself or place it in another and bet on them.
- The dumb don't question for they are sure they already have the answer.
- A computer cannot be any smarter than the person who built it.
- It's easy to find your way when you've got no place to go.
- Getting street-smart is like learning to swim in shit.
- Humor is the polite way to be honest.
- If a person is not good or talented, than only their flaws are worth discussing.
- For the most part, people defame their own character and others just spread the news.

- The people that I try to impress the hardest are my cats and they clearly find me unimpressive. The cat is the most humbling of creatures.

- If your financial walls are strong then people will lean on them.

- Aside from laziness, talent is the greatest threat to work ethic.

- Your information is only as good as the questions you ask.

- I prefer to buy gifts for needy people. I find the process easier and more gratifying.

- Many great minds come to similar conclusions the way that those who walk a narrow path trip on the same stones.

CHAPTER 3

PHILOSOPHY AND RELATED MATTERS

- I try to keep it brief because long sticks snap easier than short sticks.

- We have use for new philosophers and poets, so that the same old thing can be said with a contemporary twist, but the best of them are timeless.

- I don't think any truth is absolute. Life has a circular way about it and I find that, at best, 70 percent is the most you can shade the circle in with truth. Thirty percent of the pie will always be reserved for valid doubt. You can never make a statement that is absolutely certain for all situations. If anyone finds absolute certainty, well then, that just goes to show that even this theory is only 70 percent true in that it applies to itself.

- Things opposite to each other are defined as having a relation with each other, for they are two sides to one story.

- When you're bored, get busy before something gets busy on you.

- Infinite expands into its preexisting self.

- I write for myself and hope I have good taste.

- To want for nothing is to have everything.

- A book of logic – if it's so logical, what the fuck is the book for?

- It matters not what you think of reality for it is real if it is thought of.

- I don't like to ask questions I already know the answer to.

- I'll play the game if I am dealt a decent hand, but other than that, I would rather not be bothered.

- One of the key elements of reality is the separation of things. A master of reality finds what separates; a masterful person finds what unifies.

- We have a finite period of time to learn infinity in.
- Infinity is covered by the mind, and reality is covered by the body. Two things that exist separately with seamless joining.
- Even after all answers have been given, new questions will remain.
- We think we live in reality; when in reality, we really don't know what's really going on.
- Talk to your son born or unborn and you father yourself as well.
- I believe in lies; I just try not to live them.
- Does your infinite personality bear the face of a younger or older version of yourself?
- Balance is a seesaw that moves.
- If it's bitter make it better.
- When busy keeping your options open, remember that you cannot anchor yourself on uncertainty. While decisions make a surface for you to plant your feet on.
- It is not the purpose of life that I choose to ignore but the reason and how I pursue more.
- Money may not be able to buy happiness, but it sure can buy you a nice car to go look for it.
- I don't put much stock in beliefs because they can all be proven wrong or irrelevant; perception can bend the straightest of lines.
- Better to work on something then to get worked on.

- The thin line between love and hate cannot be erased for their mother, passion, never intended her two siblings to have to live alone and apart.

- They say it is important to settle with yourself before you can settle with someone else but now that I have settled with myself. I don't need someone else.

- Always try to answer your own question before you go asking someone else.

- Concern will keep you down. To give in to a person's concerns empowers their opinion over you.

- Sadness feels heavy for it was not meant to be carried forever.

- To explain hope, I would say, imagine one hand fills up with hope while the other fills up with shit. What hand is going to fill up faster and what do you hope will happen?

- We are born with many questions and die with little answers. The second half of your life should be spent unlearning "truth". The amount of baggage is staggering.

- Never trust someone that just wants to have sex with you, because if they cannot screw you, they will settle for screwing you over.

- The more time you spend at the edge of a cliff, the higher the odds of you falling off one.

- If you can't resolve on just one thing to write about then write a little of everything one thing at a time.

- It's the thirst for knowledge that leads to a good education, not the money spent on school.

- Live your life in a manner that when it comes down to having to eat your own words, they taste good.

- The bigger the broom, the less sweeps you have to make.

- To properly eat from the tree of knowledge, you must grow your own tree.

- If you plan to eat your whole life, then I suggest you take care of your teeth.

- If you can't be bothered by having pets, then there is a good chance that you should not bother with having children.

- You don't have to be the best to make a living.

- It is best to start out biased on a matter. A scale needs to be balanced before it can weigh in on the facts.

- Accepting truth is therapeutic, while denial is damaging.

- The key to happiness is finding comfort in boredom.

- There are vastly more good ideas then one person can think of, so don't discount everything by default.

- Speak well if you want others to care about what you say.

- The toughest thing for people who are not in pain or poverty is their emotions and feelings.

- If all infinity exists at once there would be no such thing as time, only location.

- There is no such thing as nothing.

- At this point, I don't ask about the way things work as much as I just observe, listen and think.

- The culture and values you are raised with is the first prison your mind must escape.

- If you know something for fact, you might as well stay silent on the matter but to converse about things unsure of will lead to more growth.

- *Suppose* makes the weaker side of an argument compared to *is*.

- Virtually all things will fall under contradiction with enough examination.

- Nothing comes from nothing and everything comes from the mind.

- We are all equal in that we have bodies that know suffering.

- Enlightenment is just surviving the darkness.

CHAPTER 4

PSYCHOLOGICAL

- You can tell how crazy a woman is by the way she treats her dog.

- It's a tricky matter trying to trick someone into doing something they already want to do.

- Some people go no further than from the place they start.

- The meek strive to be unique.

- He who knows everything about futility knows nothing of hope.

- Every interaction is an interaction with yourself.

- The aspects that one man likes least about another man are the qualities that a woman would like most.

- I can only listen when I've done some of the talking.

- A hungry fish will take what it can get, including the bait and the hook.

- It is easy to get lost in your subconscious for it uses your own voice.

- Confidence is a tool of the ego.

- People explain life in a manner in which their own behavior is excused.

- If you were king and the worst chair was at the head of the table, would you still sit in it?

- You can have the best time of your life while hating every minute of it.

- It is easy to be easygoing when things are going your way.

- Two people with the same shirt rarely get along at the same party.

- It is a sad epidemic that people tend to love the people that don't love them back the most.

- If fear is bad, then don't people protect what's good out of fear of losing it?

- You can't really learn your own personality till you learn someone else's first. We tend to identify ourselves with how we compare to others.

- For me, a question is all part of my examination. I don't really expect a proper answer; anything you do or don't say reveals some kind of information.

- People are happy with shit, when they don't know shit from shine.

- Our egos are something we were meant to have but not meant to use.

- The trick to getting a cat to do what you like is to just learn to like what the cat is already doing.

- Sentimentality is usually a source of downfall for it loosens one's guard.

- Men and women don't really become friends till the thrill of sleeping with each other fades, for then, there is less sexual pretense to uphold.

- One way to get insight on someone's character is to give them a small gift and see what you get in turn.

- Some people get a piece of knowledge and stick to it too hard, and it prevents them from being open enough to get another piece of knowledge.

- Giving people the benefit of the doubt is really a way to seek mercy over your own flaws.

- When asking for something that one does not wish to give, you must ask twice, for the first time you ask, they are sure to say no.

- Self-awareness is humbling for part of it entails an evaluation and acceptance of our weaknesses.

- It's not so easy to rally people to a cause that would benefit them, but for foolishness they gather by the nations.

- When someone forms an opinion, it's just an argument waiting to happen.

- The uninquisitive are never intelligent.

- Love is a reflection of the emptiness inside oneself.

- There oftentimes, an underlying implication when someone lies to you and that is that they think they are smarter than you.

- Violence is never an answer to hate for someone will not hate you less if you punch them in the face.

- Some people like themselves so much that it limits their ability to like others.

- If fear is bad, then don't people protect what's good out of fear of losing it?

- You can't really learn your own personality till you learn someone else's first. We tend to identify ourselves with how we compare to others.

- For me, a question is all part of my examination. I don't really expect a proper answer; anything you do or don't say reveals some kind of information.

- People are happy with shit, when they don't know shit from shine.

- Our egos are something we were meant to have but not meant to use.

- The trick to getting a cat to do what you like is to just learn to like what the cat is already doing.

- Sentimentality is usually a source of downfall for it loosens one's guard.

- Men and women don't really become friends till the thrill of sleeping with each other fades, for then, there is less sexual pretense to uphold.

- One way to get insight on someone's character is to give them a small gift and see what you get in turn.

- Some people get a piece of knowledge and stick to it too hard, and it prevents them from being open enough to get another piece of knowledge.

- Giving people the benefit of the doubt is really a way to seek mercy over your own flaws.

- When asking for something that one does not wish to give, you must ask twice, for the first time you ask, they are sure to say no.

- Self-awareness is humbling for part of it entails an evaluation and acceptance of our weaknesses.

- It's not so easy to rally people to a cause that would benefit them, but for foolishness they gather by the nations.

- When someone forms an opinion, it's just an argument waiting to happen.

- The uninquisitive are never intelligent.

- Love is a reflection of the emptiness inside oneself.

- There oftentimes, an underlying implication when someone lies to you and that is that they think they are smarter than you.

- Violence is never an answer to hate for someone will not hate you less if you punch them in the face.

- Some people like themselves so much that it limits their ability to like others.

CHAPTER 5

GOD AND RELIGION

- Love thy neighbors as you love thy self or love thy self as you love your neighbors.

- In the Middle East, one does not need to look for a church for over there, the church finds you.

- You are in charge of your own soul, and your soul is currency for the universe, so spend it wisely.

- The ideal man taught us not to worship idols.

- The church favors itself as being a business over being a lifestyle.

- The devil wears loose clothes but his demons hold on to them tightly.

- God speaks and interacts with us all, but like us, he dons a mask or an act, you could say. He likes to start off by acting like the devil as some sort of interview procedure he conducts before he allows you to get near him.

- God has more effect on things watched less closely.

- God made us to do the things he cannot and installed a sense of mysticism over the things he does.

- People have the tendency of listening to God while dancing with the devil.

- Christians don't want to forgive; they just want their sins to be forgiven.

- I'm at my best when talking to myself and I have the most wonderful conversations. There is a part of God within all of us and we communicate with him through ourselves.

- Living gods and prophets are a threat to the priesthood. They only have use for the dead and martyred.

- If everyone were to switch to Buddhism or some kind of monkhood, who would be left to receive all the possessions that need be given away?

- For every bird that flies in heaven, is there a fish that swims in hell?

- Seek not God's love for you already have it.

- You don't get out of hell till ya been bit by a dog and scratched by a cat.

- Many people can't think past the basic options presented them by others. This is how religion catches on to the mainstream.

- Better to grow your own grapes then to count on Jesus to come along and touch your water.

- Anyone who makes a good Chicken Parmesan is a saint.

- The Jews were a tribal cult that took over the world with their invention of Christianity, which they were wise enough to avoid.

- You have to pay temple dues to get a Jewish upbringing. It's like being born into a workers' union.

- Who holds the Word of God? The poet or the prophet? If there be a God, how would you expect him to speak if not eloquent?

- The only thing that would make the Bible plausible is that truth is stranger than fiction.

- The truth lives in the present, past and future with or without mankind and if earth humans stop spreading the word of Jesus, he would never be discovered again.

CHAPTER 6

SHORT STORIES

HARD HEADS

So, two guys with hard heads meet each other. One guy says to the other: "Hey, since you have a hard head and I have a hard head, let's put our heads together and see what we can figure out."

So they start to smash their heads together, with neither one giving way. They stop at one point and one decides to speak up first, and he says, "I guess we figured out that we got some hard heads." The other guys says: "Man I have just been waiting for you to say that this whole time."

THE JUGGLER

A star baseball pitcher is in the closing moments of a game. He throws a fastball and gets the last out to win the game. After he cleans up, he meets up with his girlfriend, and they start to make their way through the crowd of fans.

When they reach some clear space, past the initial crowd, they see another crowd is forming around a man that is juggling baseballs. The pitcher's girlfriend grabs him by the hand and says: "Let's go check it out." They walk over and join the crowd of onlookers. As the juggler spots the pitcher, he stops juggling and tells the crowd: "Excuse me for a moment, my favorite player just walked up, and I want to get his autograph."

As the player hears this, he walks up to the juggler, and the juggler hands him one of his balls for the player to sign. After the player hands back the ball, he asks the juggler: "How do you juggle?"

The juggler tells him: "Anything I can do, you can do."

The player then says: "I still cannot juggle."

The juggler then says: "Let me correct myself, anything you can do, I can do."

The player then says: "I still cannot juggle."

The juggler replies: "Well, it was nice to meet you but I am sticking to my story since you are sticking to your story."

The baseball player then returns to the crowd and stands next to his girlfriend. The juggler begins to juggle again.

As everyone stares in awe, the girl leans into her man's arms but he takes little notice of her because he is concentrating on watching the act while trying to figure out how the man juggles. After a short while, the juggler begins to get bored because the juggling is nothing to him, he was just born able to do it. So the juggler starts to think of a way he can end his act. After giving it some thought, the juggler asks the crowd for a brave volunteer to step forward.

As he says this, the girl looks into her boyfriend's eyes and as soon as their eyes lock, he finally takes notice of her and shoves her forward. As soon as the juggler spots the movement, he instantly drops all the balls but one and throws a baseball-style fastball and hits the girl right in the leg. As she falls down, crying in pain, everyone is stunned.

As the ball rolls away, the player picks it up and spots his signature and gets angry, yelling at the juggler, "Yo! You're a real asshole for doing that. What's stopping me from throwing this ball even harder than you and you get knocked the fuck out?"

The juggler quickly says, "Oh, so you can do what I can do."

www.ingramcontent.com/pod-product-compliance
Lightning Source LLC
Chambersburg PA
CBHW021431070526
44577CB00001B/156